MW01227030

# U.S. ★ WARPLANES

# THE B-1 LANCER

**Amy Sterling Casil**

the rosen publishing group's
rosen
central

*To Col. Bob Baldwin, USAF Ret.,*
*the best boss a young person ever had*

Published in 2003 by The Rosen Publishing Group, Inc.
29 East 21st Street, New York, NY 10010

First Edition

### Library of Congress Cataloging-in-Publication Data

Casil, Amy Sterling.
The B-1 Lancer / Amy Sterling Casil.— 1st ed.
    p. cm. — (U.S. warplanes)
Summary: An examination of the machinery, specifications, technology,
and capabilities of the B-1B with a discussion of the plane's early
development, combat history, and likely future.
Includes bibliographical references and index.
ISBN 0-8239-3871-9 (library binding)
1. B-1 bomber—Juvenile literature. [1. B-1 bomber. 2. Bombers.]
I. Title. II. Series.
UG1242.B6 C38 2003
623.7'463—dc21

                                   2002007770

*Manufactured in the United States of America*

# CONTENTS

On September 11, 2001, people around the world watched in horror as two hijacked U.S. airliners crashed into the twin towers of the World Trade Center in New York City, both of which collapsed soon after. A short time later, a third hijacked plane crashed into the Pentagon in Arlington, Virginia (just outside Washington, D.C.), and a fourth plane, possibly on its way to the White House or the Capitol, went down in a field in western Pennsylvania after a group of passengers struggled for control over the plane with the hijackers. More than 3,000 people were killed as a result of the four hijackings, and many others were injured.

The hijackers are believed to have been part of the Al Qaeda terrorist organization led by a Saudi Arabian exile named Osama bin Laden. This organization is dedicated to removing the presence and influence of the United States and other Western nations in Islamic lands.

The north tower of the World Trade Center collapses into smoldering rubble after terrorists, believed to be associated with Al Qaeda, crashed airplanes into the complex on September 11, 2001. The south tower had collapsed twenty-three minutes earlier.

Smoke rises from caves, alleged to have been hideouts for Taliban and Al Qaeda soldiers, after being bombed by U.S. warplanes such as the B-1B. The United States's response to the September 11 attacks was swift and powerful, sweeping the ruling Taliban from power in Afghanistan and sending Al Qaeda forces on the run. Nevertheless, terrorist mastermind and Al Qaeda leader, Osama bin Laden, apparently escaped, and the manhunt continued for many months.

Al Qaeda's base of operations was in Afghanistan, an Islamic country long torn by war and poverty. Afghanistan is a mountainous land east of Iran and west of Pakistan. Soon after September 11, 2001, U.S. president George W. Bush declared a "war on terror." Osama bin Laden and his associates had set up many terrorist training camps in Afghanistan, and it was thought that many members of Al Qaeda, including bin Laden, were still hiding out in the country's vast network of caves and mountains. So Afghanistan was selected by President Bush and the U.S. military as the first target of their new worldwide offensive to wipe out terrorism. The United States, wary of appearing to act alone against a weaker Islamic adversary, formed a coalition of over thirty other countries who were also committed to the war on terrorism and contributed in various ways.

While the ongoing war on terror is designed to stop deadly terrorists in their tracks, it is never acceptable to kill innocent civilians. Because terrorists live and operate undetected among the general population, launching an attack on them poses a high risk of innocent people getting caught in the cross fire. With every civilian death caused by military error, international support for the war on terror weakens, especially among Islamic countries. So, more than ever before, the use of precision weapons and accurate intelligence information is crucial.

The U.S. military is using high-tech reconnaissance, fighters, bombers, and armament—bombs and missiles—to try to make sure that innocent people are not harmed. Because of its long-range and high-tech capabilities, the B-1B bomber is one of the most important weapons in the war on terror. The B-1B is a long-range, multirole, heavy bomber with a top speed of more than 900 miles per hour (1,440 km/hr). It carries a crew of four, fires short-range attack missiles, and releases many different types of precision-guided bombs and cruise missiles.

Since the days when the B-1B bomber was no more than a design idea, the plane has been the subject of controversy—for its expense, its weaponry, and its performance. Even after finally joining the ranks of the U.S. Air Force's warplanes—more than thirty years after it was first proposed—the B-1B was not given a chance to prove its critics wrong. It did not fly a single combat mission until more than fourteen years after the U.S. Air Force first put it into active duty. Today, however, it shares a place of honor as the United States's first line of defense against international terrorism.

# THE HISTORY OF THE B-1

The B-1 bomber program was conceived in the midst of super-power conflict. But it was born into controversy at home that took more than twenty years to resolve. The B-1 Lancer has existed under a cloud of doubt ever since it was just an idea on paper. Only recently has it finally had a chance to show what it can do and prove its critics wrong.

The B-1 bomber program was the product of the longest aircraft development effort in history. The road to the Lancer's active military service was a winding one, marked by many obstacles, setbacks, and changes of mission.

## *The Cold War*

The B-1 project can be traced back to 1962 when the U.S. Department of Defense began searching for a new airborne component for the country's nuclear defense forces. The United States was at the height of the Cold War with the former Soviet Union (which broke up in the early 1990s into Russia and other independent countries, such as Lithuania and Ukraine). The Cold War got its name because it never "heated up." No real battles were ever fought directly by the super-powers, though the tensions were often high, especially with thousands of nuclear missiles pointed at each country.

This strained, dangerous peace lasted from shortly after World War II to 1991, when the last Soviet leader, Mikhail Gorbachev, resigned. With breathtaking suddenness, seventy-four years of Communist rule ended for the former Soviet Union and the entire Eastern Bloc (the nations of Eastern Europe that were under the Soviet Union's control).

The fall of the Berlin Wall in 1989 was a potent symbol of the end of Communism in Eastern Europe. For years, the fortified concrete and wire barrier had stood as the dividing line not only between East and West Germany but also between freedom and democracy and the closed and repressive governments of the Communist Eastern Bloc.

"Strategy" was the key word for the United States in its defense against Cold War enemies. A by-product of Cold War strategy was a very expensive arms race. Both superpowers spent billions of dollars building weapons—such as ships, submarines, missiles, bombs, and warplanes—in order to gain military superiority or at least make the other side think long and hard about the consequences before attacking. The B-1 bomber was an important part of this arms race.

The B-1 was designed to be a long-range, strategic bomber. That meant that it could strike deep in the heart of the Soviet Union and drop nuclear weapons. From the start, however, it was clear that the B-1 would put an enormous economic strain on the resources of the U.S. military. The four B-1A prototypes (fully operational models used for testing) developed by Rockwell International (now Boeing) quickly became controversial because of their high cost and elaborate nuclear technology,

Dignitaries, politicians, and workers marvel at the prototype of the B-1 bomber during a rollout ceremony at the Rockwell International Hanger in Palmdale, California, on October 26, 1974. At the time, the B-1 bomber was the most expensive weapons system in history, a fact that drew criticism from many quarters and almost led to the scrapping of the plane's development.

which many people considered unnecessary. The initial cost of each plane—$280 million—was so expensive that comedians joked that the plane was the "B-1 Bummer." In 1977, President Jimmy Carter canceled the program. The money saved was instead put toward buying cruise missiles like the ALCM (air launched cruise missile), SRAM (short range attack missile), and Tomahawk, which are still used today.

Just when it looked like the B-1 bomber was dead, a new president took office, and suddenly the Lancer got a second lease on life. In 1981, President Ronald Reagan restarted the program. Luckily, the U.S. Air Force had never stopped testing the four prototypes it had received from Rockwell. Even though the bomber was still controversial, Rockwell received a contract to build 100 B-1B Lancers, an improved version of the original plane design, which was now referred to as the B-1A. The first B-1B was delivered to the U.S. Air

## THE B-1A

The B-1A was the original prototype version of the B-1 bomber. Only four B-1As were built between 1974 and 1977 as test prototypes. Although it looks similar to the B-1B on the outside, aviation experts say that on the inside they are two completely different planes. B-1B improvements and modifications included new radar, new generation computers, a window for the offensive and defensive systems officers' stations, precision weapon delivery, and structural changes to reduce exposure to enemy radar. The B-1B also has a higher takeoff weight capacity, allowing it to carry more weapons. With a maximum speed of 1,390 mph (2,224 km/hr), however, the B-1A was a faster aircraft than the B-1B (which can fly at only about 900 mph, or 1,440 km/hr). The original four prototypes were never flown during combat missions; they were used only as test aircraft.

Force in June 1985 and was fully operational by October 1, 1986. The final B-1B was delivered on May 2, 1988.

## *The Controversy Continues*

The B-1B was designed to take some of the load off of the aging warhorse, the mighty B-52 bomber, which had been in service since World War II. Yet before the Lancer could fill that role, it had to undertake another sort of campaign—an all-out political fight for survival. The huge plane has often had trouble gaining support in Congress, which sets the military budget and directs how money will be spent.

Critics opposed the B-1B because it was extremely expensive— each of the fifty-one B-1Bs currently in service cost more than $200 million to build. They said that it lacked "stealth" radar technology (a design that allows planes to escape the notice of enemy radar) as advanced as the newer and more expensive B-2 bomber. It was also said to be less reliable than the B-52, a plane with a much longer combat history and simpler technology that required less maintenance. There were reports that the B-1s suffered from cracked landing gears, leaking fuel tanks, and faulty engines that fell off of the

# THE B-1B AT A GLANCE

Primary function: Long-range, multirole, heavy bomber

Builder: Boeing, North America (formerly Rockwell International, North American Aircraft)

Power plant: Four General Electric F-101-GE-102 turbofan engines with afterburners

Thrust: 30,000-plus pounds (13,608 kg) with afterburner, per engine

Length: 146 feet (44.5 meters)

Wingspan: 137 feet (41.8 meters) extended forward; 79 feet (24.1 meters) swept aft

Height: 34 feet (10.4 meters)

Weight when empty: 190,000 pounds (86,183 kg)

Maximum takeoff weight: 477,000 pounds (216,634 kg)

Speed: 900-plus mph (1,440 km/hr; Mach 1.2 at sea level)

Range: Intercontinental without refueling; 7,455 miles (11,998 km)

Ceiling: Above 30,000 feet (9,144 meters)

Crew: Four (aircraft commander, copilot, offensive systems officer, and defensive systems officer)

Weapons: Three internal weapons bays can accommodate up to eighty-four Mk-82 general purpose bombs or Mk-62 naval mines, thirty CBU-87/89 cluster munitions or CBU-97 Sensor Fused Weapons, and twenty-four GBU-31 JDAM guided bombs or Mk-84 general purpose bombs

First deployed: June 1985

Cost per plane: $200 million plus

Inventory: Total of ninety-two B-1Bs, fifty-one in active service

*Source: USAF B-1B Lancer Fact Sheet*

A B-52 Stratofortress taking off from RAF Fairford, United Kingdom, on a combat mission over Yugoslavia in May 1999. After close to fifty years, albeit with considerable upgrading, the B-52 remains one of the most impressive U.S. warplanes. Capable of launching the widest array of weapons in the United States's inventory, the heavy bomber has been used in World War II, Operation Desert Storm, and, most recently, Operation Enduring Freedom in Afghanistan.

planes' bodies. Onboard alarms were said to go off for no reason. The bombers broke down often and were rarely combat ready. Maintenance was extremely expensive, and there was not enough money to keep spare parts in stock. At any given time, as much as half the fleet of B-1Bs were out of service due to maintenance problems. By the early 1990s, its critics were again calling for a complete halt to the B-1 program.

## A New Mission

Strangely enough for a plane born of superpower aggression, it was the end of the Cold War that gave the B-1B new life. Throughout the 1990s, the B-1B received new upgrades and adaptations that would allow it to carry conventional bombs—rather than nuclear bombs—because the threat of nuclear warfare was greatly reduced after the collapse of the Soviet Union and the increasing closeness of the United States and Russia. In fact, a treaty called START (Strategic Arms Reduction Treaty) signed by the Soviet Union and the United States in 1991 (and reaffirmed by Russia and other former Soviet republics in 1993) prevented the B-1B from carrying nuclear weapons.

While taking away its nuclear weapons would seem to leave the B-1B without a mission, it in fact made the plane more versatile to the U.S. Air Force. As part of its Conventional Mission Upgrade program (which is discussed in detail in chapter 2), the U.S. Air Force began a series of improvements that would greatly expand the bomber's abilities and possible activities. These improvements have helped turn the B-1B into a powerful weapon that now serves as the backbone of the U.S. long-range bomber fleet.

U.S. president George Herbert Walker Bush *(left)* and his Russian counterpart, President Boris Yeltsin, close the deal on the START-2 treaty in Russia on January 3, 1993. In signing the treaty, President Bush reaffirmed the United States's commitment not to use the B-1 bomber to launch nuclear weapons.

# 2 THE NUTS AND BOLTS OF THE B-1B

Though long criticized as expensive and unreliable, the B-1B Lancer is a marvel of high-tech engineering. Because it was held up for so long by political and budgetary controversies, it rarely had a chance to show what it could do. Only after its successful performances in Iraq in 1998, Kosovo in 1999, and Afghanistan in 2001–2002 has an accurate picture of the bomber's abilities begun to emerge. Now many U. S. Air Force pilots, politicians, and the public are beginning to realize that they may have gotten their money's worth after all.

## Stealth Technology

While the B-1B's formal name is the Lancer (for its sleek, pointed design and arsenal of destructive weapons), the plane is also called the Bone because of its name (B-One) and its long, lean shape. At about two-thirds the size of its older "sister" bomber, the B-52, the B-1B has only one-hundredth the radar cross-section of the big, lumbering B-52, thanks to its unique construction. Because of its smooth and narrow design and use of radar-absorbing materials, the B-1B has very little surface area exposed to radar detection, making it very difficult for the bomber to be picked up on enemy radar. This makes it a "stealthy" bomber, one that is almost invisible in flight.

This "invisibility" is further enhanced by the B-1B's defensive avionics. The Lancer includes electronics that allow it to jam enemy radar that would detect and guide missiles or anti-aircraft fire toward the bomber. The Lancer can also fire decoys, such as flares, to further confuse enemy radar.

These aerial views of a B-1B Lancer in flight over farm fields show its swing wings swept back *(right)* and spread wide. Swing wings make a plane heavier and more difficult to command, but the ability to change wing positions gives the plane the flexibility to achieve supersonic speed, land on relatively short runways, and reduce fuel consumption.

## Swing Wings

The B-1B bomber is a "swing wing" aircraft. That means that its wings can be fixed in a swept forward position or moved back, depending on the plane's mission and flight pattern. During takeoff, landing, and high-altitude cruising, the wings are swept forward at almost a right angle to the bomber's body. When flying above or close to supersonic speeds (faster than the speed of sound), the wings are moved back, giving the bomber greater maneuverability at high speed. The crew can change the direction of the wings in flight by using a lever near the copilot's seat.

## The Lancer in Flight

The B-1B can fly at Mach 1.2 at sea level, or more than 900 miles per hour (1,440 km/hr). Mach 1 is the speed of sound. Mach 2 is twice the speed of sound. Its flight ceiling, or the maximum height it can fly safely, is 30,000 feet (9,144 meters) high in the stratosphere. It can fly from Los Angeles to New York in four hours, at only 200 feet (70 meters) above the ground, without having to stop to refuel.

The B-1B flies this high thanks to four General Electric F-101-GE-102 turbofan engines with afterburners. Each of these engines produces more than 30,000 pounds (13,608 kg) of thrust (force of acceleration). This is almost twice the power of the engines used by the U.S. Navy's top fighter plane, the F/A-18 Hornet, the ultrafast plane flown by the Blue Angels. Afterburners are devices placed in the tailpipe of a turbojet engine that provide extra thrust by injecting fuel into the engine's exhaust gases. This gives the Lancer more power during takeoffs, landings, and high-speed maneuvers.

## Weapons

The B-1B no longer carries nuclear weapons. As a result, it can now carry a much more varied payload of bombs and missiles, allowing it to fly in many different kinds of missions.

These weapons are stored in forward, intermediate, and aft (rear) weapons bays. Weapons bays are the places in the airplane's long body where the bombs and missiles are stored and from which they are eventually dropped or fired. The bays can carry bombs or missiles, or even be converted to carry extra fuel for ultra long-range missions (although the B-1B usually refuels during flight with the help of KC-135 Stratotanker refueling planes). A movable bulkhead (a wall that separates compartments) between the front and middle compartments makes the weapons bays extremely versatile. The three bays can be combined into two to carry extra bombs or special payloads. The B-1B can carry more bombs than the B-52 bomber. In fact, it has the largest internal weapons payload of any current bomber.

On the outside of the bomber, under its fuselage (the central body of the plane that contains the crew and weapons), are six

A B-1B Lancer is refueled during flight by a KC-135 Stratotanker. Not having to land for refueling allows the Lancer to engage in long-range missions and reach its targets far more quickly and efficiently.

additional external hardpoints (weapon mounts) that can hold additional bombs and missiles. The maximum internal weapons payload (the bombs and missiles stored in the internal weapons bays) is 75,000 pounds (34,019 kg). The maximum external weapons payload (the bombs and missiles mounted on the hardpoints) is 59,000 pounds (26,762 kg).

The internal weapons bays can carry the AGM-86B air launched cruise missile (ALCM; a radar-guided conventional missile that flies as far as 1,562.5 miles [2,500 km] at low altitude and delivers an explosion of 200 kilotons), the AGM-69 short-range attack missile (a nuclear missile that is no longer permitted on the B-1B), and the joint direct attack munition (JDAM). JDAM is a satellite-guided system that can deliver 1,000–2,000 pound (453–907 kg) bombs within thirteen meters of their target. The external hardpoints can also carry the AGM-86B ALCM. The prefix AGM stands for air-to-ground missile.

The Lancer is the only U.S. bomber capable of carrying twenty-four of the special JDAM bombs at once. It can also carry eighty-four conventional unguided bombs and a dozen special joint standoff weapon (JSOW) missiles that rely on their own radar to hit targets with pinpoint accuracy.

---

## "J" IS FOR "JOINT"

Why do the U.S. armed forces start the names of so many of their weapons with "J," like JDAM and JSOW? "J" stands for "joint," which means that all branches of the armed forces are able to use the weapon. In the past, the U.S. Army, Navy, Air Force, and Marines used weapons unique to each branch. Today, cooperation is the key, with flexible weapons systems that can be used in the air, on land, and in the water.

---

## The Ride

Another unique aspect of the B-1B bomber is its control system. A yoke or steering wheel–type system guides other bombers. The B-1B uses a joystick similar to the ones used by fighter jets. As a result, it handles more like a fighter than a bomber when in flight. Pilots report that the B-1B can do a 360-degree roll like a fighter, but the Pentagon will not confirm their statements.

## In the Cockpit

The flight commander and copilot are seated in the front of the cockpit, while the offensive and defensive systems officers are seated to their rear down a walkway, closer to the weapons bays. All areas of the cockpit and systems controls are filled with the most up-to-date avionics equipment and displays.

The offensive systems officer oversees the offensive avionics system (OAS). This system includes a variety of radar that allows the crew to adjust the aircraft's position without using ground-based navigation aids, update mission information, pinpoint the coordinates of possible enemy targets, and deliver bombs and missiles with precision.

The defensive systems officer oversees the defensive avionics system (DAS). This system includes electronic jamming equipment, radar location and warning systems, radio surveillance, and a towed decoy system. The radar and warning systems help the B-1B locate nearby enemies and prepare to take the appropriate defensive measures. The jamming equipment enables the Lancer to interfere with enemy radar, making the bomber far harder to detect. Flares and towed decoys are used to confuse enemy radar and draw heat-seeking missiles safely away from the bomber.

Because the B-1B is designed for long-range, strategic missions, the crew can spend many hours on board, with some missions lasting between twelve and sixteen continuous hours.

## The Conventional Mission Upgrade Program

When the Cold War ended, the B-1B suddenly seemed like a plane without a mission. The U.S. Air Force, hesitant to scrap a plane that had taken so long and cost so much to develop, tried to find ways to adapt the bomber to new military realities. A series of upgrades and modifications were made that transformed the B-1B's mission from that of a long-range nuclear bomber (in the old B-52 mold) to one that could provide massive and rapid delivery of precision and non-precision conventional weapons against any target, anywhere, on very short notice.

The most important upgrades have been achieved as a result of the air force's Conventional Mission Upgrade Program. This program has allowed the B-1B to transform itself into a conventional bomber, with a varied payload of precision and nonprecision missiles and bombs. As a result, by 2003, the Lancer will be able to drop cluster bombs, satellite-guided JDAM bombs and missiles, JSOWs, and joint air-to-surface standoff missiles (JASSMs). Under this program, the Lancer's defenses will also be upgraded, including the towed decoy system, improved electronic jamming equipment, and secure radios

**The Lancer has the capability to drop cluster bombs. B-1B aircrews use the plane's radar equipment to aim at targets in flight without the need for land-based navigational aids.**

that allow for communication between planes and the ground that cannot be intercepted by the enemy. Defensive radar and computerized communications systems have also been improved.

Because of these upgrades, the B-1Bs of tomorrow will be as different from the B-1Bs of today as the B-1B is from the original prototype B-1A test planes. Colonel Ben F. McCarter, B-1B system program office director, told the *Los Angeles Times*, "With the Conventional Mission Upgrade Program, no other weapon system will be able to match the B-1B's combination of speed, range, lethality, and cost-effectiveness."

Thirteen years after the first B-1B was delivered to the U.S. Air Force, the "new" bomber finally got its first chance to prove itself in combat, flying successful missions over Iraq in 1998.

Now that the B-1B has gotten the chance to fly real combat missions—more than thirty-five years after it was first conceived—by most accounts it has done a great job. Military experts call it the star player in Afghanistan.

Yet despite these recent and long overdue successes, serious questions remain about the Lancer's safety record and cost. Even though often referred to as the backbone of the United States's long-range bomber force, a familiar cloud of doubt still hangs over the B-1B.

## The Lancer's Debut

The B-1B flew its first combat missions in Operation Desert Fox in Iraq in 1998. Its goal was to strike military and security targets that contribute to Iraq's ability to produce, store, maintain, and deliver weapons of mass destruction.

Though designed as a long-range nuclear bomber, the Lancer has never carried nuclear bombs in any mission. Against Iraq, it carried conventional bombs. B-1Bs flew four missions there and hit three targets, including Iraqi army barracks. They dropped more than 150,000 pounds (68,039 kg) of weapons during the four-day operation.

A year later, during Operation Allied Force—designed to damage the Serbian military and security forces that Yugoslavian president Slobodan Milosevic had used to murder and terrorize members of the Albanian majority in Kosovo—Lancers flew 100 missions and delivered 5,033 weapons weighing a total of 2.5 million pounds (1.14 million kg).

Aircraft maintenance personnel perform a technical check on a U.S. Air Force B-1B Lancer from Ellsworth AFB, South Dakota, at its forward deployment base in the United Kingdom before loading it with conventional and cluster bombs. This plane, and the weapons in the forefront of the photograph, were used during NATO airstrikes on Yugoslavia in April 1999.

During this four-month operation, B-1Bs dropped 19 percent of the bombs used against Serbian targets, which included runways, military facilities, and equipment.

## Operation Enduring Freedom

In peacetime, the Lancer is stationed at five specialized air force bases around the United States: Mountain Home Air Force Base (AFB) in Idaho, Ellsworth AFB in South Dakota, McConnell AFB in Kansas, Dyess AFB in Texas, and Robins AFB in Georgia. When the United States is involved in an armed conflict, such as Operation Enduring Freedom in Afghanistan, the B-1B must be "staged" from (stationed at) U.S.- or NATO-controlled air bases near the conflict because of its constant need for repair and maintenance. The nearest base to Afghanistan is the island of Diego Garcia in the Indian Ocean.

An air force B-1B crew chief gives an all-clear sign to the pilot of a Lancer flying a combat mission on January 3, 2002, during Operation Enduring Freedom.

A B-1B Lancer takes off from the island of Diego Garcia in the Indian Ocean for a combat mission in support of Operation Enduring Freedom. During the military offensive, Lancers bombed targets such as warning radars, airfields, and Al Qaeda and Taliban cave complexes and command facilities in Afghanistan.

During Operation Enduring Freedom, eight of America's B-1Bs were stationed on Diego Garcia and flew up to four sorties (bombing missions) per day against terrorist hideouts in Afghanistan. These B-1Bs carried the AGM-86 air-launched cruise missile, which has a range of over 1,500 miles (2,400 km) and uses a global positioning system (GPS)—a satellite guidance system—to hit targets with extreme accuracy. Ordinary bombs can be converted to super-accurate weapons using the JDAM system that makes bombs "smart" (a smart bomb is a bomb that can respond to target location information provided by troops on the ground, a B-1B cockpit crew, or a GPS satellite). The JDAM, like the Tomahawk cruise missile, uses the GPS to direct it straight to its target.

In Afghanistan, Al Qaeda terrorists and the Taliban leadership that was protecting them tried to hide in a dense network of caves high in isolated mountains. B-1B bombers flew missions that sent JDAM bombs and

# LOST LANCERS

Since the B-1 program began, eight Lancers have been lost as a result of accidents.

★ **August 29, 1984:** Crash during the aircraft's development program. Cause: Loss of control of aircraft during a center of gravity test of the bomber's aft. One test pilot died when the parachute system of his ejection module malfunctioned. Two other crew members in the same module survived.

★ **September 28, 1987:** Crash near Pueblo, Colorado, during a low-level training mission. Cause: The plane struck a twenty-pound (nine kg) white pelican, which tore through the bomber's wing; destroyed important hydraulic, electrical, and fuel lines; and started a fire. One crew member died when his ejection seat malfunctioned. Two instructors who did not have ejection seats and did not have time to bail out manually also died. Three other crew members ejected safely. This was the first B-1B crash after the aircraft became operational in 1986.

★ **November 8, 1988:** Crash at Dyess AFB, Texas, during practice landings. Cause: A fire in the left wing knocked out two of the plane's four engines and burned out important control equipment. All four crewmen parachuted to safety.

★ **November 17, 1988:** Crash on approach to runway at Ellsworth AFB, South Dakota. Cause: Pilot error. All four crewmen ejected safely.

★ **November 30, 1992:** Crash near Van Horn, Texas, during a routine low-level night flight. Cause: Pilot error. All four crew members were killed.

★ **September 19, 1997:** Crash near Alzada, Montana, during a training mission. Cause: An excessively rapid descent during an authorized and routine defensive maneuver. All four crew members were killed.

★ **February 18, 1998:** Crash near Marion, Kentucky, during a low-level training mission. Cause: A short circuit that shut down all four engines. All four crew members ejected safely.

★ **December 12, 2001:** Crash in the Indian Ocean near the Diego Garcia air base during Operation Enduring Freedom. Cause: Multiple malfunctions. All four crew members ejected safely.

*Source: GlobalSecurity.org*

AGM-86 smart missiles straight into their hideouts. As Operation Enduring Freedom wound down, it was reported that fewer than 100 Al Qaeda and Taliban fighters remained in this area, down from many thousands. Lancers also delivered precision bombs in support of allied ground troops, allowing them to win every major ground battle fought in the war.

The B-1B dropped almost 4 million pounds (1.8 million kg) of bombs on Afghanistan and carried 60 percent of the bomber load, flying 150 sorties from the joint U.S./British base on Diego Garcia. Given how remote and mountainous Afghanistan is, the success of the relatively untested B-1B is dramatic. Lancers have flown thousands of miles to drop their bombs on Afghan targets with an accuracy of within a few feet. Just one B-1B was able to drop ten smart bombs on a compound in Afghanistan where senior leaders of Al Qaeda and the Taliban were gathered for a meeting.

The Lancer is "finally getting the opportunity to prove its capabilities, which we knew it had when we built it," Charles "Bill" Bright, who was the original B-1B flight test manager, told the *Los Angeles Times*. Now the first choice of U.S. military leadership, and proven in combat in Afghanistan, the B-1B is poised to live up to its potential and fly into the future defending the nation against terrorism and any other threats.

## Lingering Doubts

Despite the B-1B's upgrades—which have made it a more versatile and stealthier bomber—and its combat successes, very serious doubts about the bomber's future remain. The old complaints about the high cost of maintaining the B-1B, the lack of spare parts, and the fleet's low combat-ready percentage are still being voiced. Some experts estimate that every B-1B flight hour costs as much as $12,000 in maintenance. As a result, some maintenance may not be able to be performed. In July 2001, the U.S. Air Force secretary reported that the B-1 program was $2 billion short of what it needed for scheduled upgrades.

In addition to these familiar complaints, newer concerns about the Lancer's safety have arisen in the wake of a B-1B crash in the Indian

Ocean in December 2001. In that crash, the pilot reported that the bomber experienced multiple malfunctions that made it uncontrollable. This fits into a pattern of breakdowns that have brought down eight Lancers since the B-1 program began and have led to dozens of less serious "mishaps." Most of these have been blamed on engine problems, collisions with birds, hydraulic system problems, landing gear damage, and pilot error.

The Lancer now has the highest mishap rate of any aircraft in the air force's bomber fleet (3.26 serious incidents for every 100,000 hours flown) and ranks third among all air force aircraft. This is a partly mislead-

This undated photo shows B-1B bombers under construction at the Rockwell International assembly plant in Palmdale, California.

ing statistic, however. Because it flies far more than either the B-52 or B-2, the Lancer is more likely to have an accident. While the twenty-one B-2 stealth bombers flew only 30,249 hours in 2000, the ninety-two B-1Bs flew 368,177 hours.

## *Improving Safety*

It seems like the tide may be turning for the B-1B, however. Between 2000 and 2001, the bomber's reported mishaps declined dramatically, from twenty-eight to eight. An aircraft's early years are often marked by malfunctions and crashes. Over time—with mechanical and structural improvements and greater pilot experience—the mishap rate often levels off.

A weapons load crew places a conventional bomb rack onto a B-1B Lancer at a Royal Air Force base in Fairford, England. Lancers and support personnel from the 28th Bomb Wing stationed at Ellsworth Air Force Base, South Dakota, were deployed to England to support NATO's Operation Allied Force.

# 4 THE CREW

Aviation professionals, from aircraft mechanics to pilots to systems officers, all say that flying is in the blood. They are all proud of the planes they build, maintain, and fly. Their opinions on an aircraft's performance and quality, therefore, carry a lot of weight. They are the ones—not politicians, journalists, or bureaucrats—who are intimately familiar with the planes and how they fly. Though the B-1B has had more than its share of critics, it enjoys great popularity among pilots and crews.

## *Education and Training*

The first step to becoming an air force pilot for any type of plane is to earn a commission, which means becoming an officer. There are three ways to earn a commission. You can be appointed to the Air Force Academy, which is a college for those interested in entering the air force. If you cannot get into the Air Force Academy, you can join the Reserve Officer Training Corps (ROTC) at the college you attend. If you are currently in college or if you have already graduated, your only remaining option is to enlist in the air force and attend officer training school (OTS). No matter which route pilots choose, upon graduation they are commissioned as a second lieutenant in the air force.

After commissioning, people who want to be pilots attend the Air Education and Training Command (AETC), with headquarters at Randolph Air Force Base near San Antonio, Texas. The AETC recruits new people into the air force and provides them with military, technical, and flight training, as well as professional, military, and continuing education.

## NOSE ART

The B-1B has a long nose with the cockpit set in front of the aircraft, which gives it a distinctive look, like a bird of prey. Since the days of World War I biplanes, colorful artwork painted on the aircraft (today referred to as nose art) has served to inspire professional pride in the pilots and crews who both fly and maintain airplanes in time of war. B-1Bs are painted with nose art that pays tribute to the courage of their service units with themes like "Thunder from the Sky" and shows a sense of humor with titles like "Home Improvement." Many B-1Bs are painted with warlike images of fighting tigers, skulls, black widow spiders, and eagles.

Other flight crew and ground crew—from weapons systems officers to technical personnel—also join the air force and receive basic training. If people want to work in any way on the B-1B bomber, even if they do not want to be pilots, they will have to attend the AETC. After receiving basic training and before they start their air force jobs, enlisted people are trained in technical skills, such as communications, satellite technology, and aircraft maintenance and avionics.

B-1B pilots and weapons systems personnel receive more advanced training at the B-1B "schoolhouse," located at Dyess AFB

Air force cadets march in formation during a ceremony at the U.S. Air Force Academy in Colorado Springs, Colorado. Not all cadets will become top-gun pilots. Because the warplanes are so expensive and require great skill and nerves of steel, only a select few will survive the rigorous screening and training process.

in Texas. Laughlin AFB in Texas, Columbus AFB in Missouri, and Vance AFB in Oklahoma are the three other bases where special B-1B training programs are held.

Once enlisted personnel and officers receive their training and are selected as flight or ground crew for the B-1B bomber, they are stationed at one of five main bases where the B-1B is flown. They become part of a bomber "wing," which is the air force term for the group of planes, pilots, and crew who work at and fly out of these bases.

## Expert Opinions

B-1B mechanics have a love/hate relationship with the plane. Technical Sergeant Daniel Hutson, 9th Bomb Squadron, told *Airman* magazine that the challenge of keeping the B-1B in smooth working order is its sheer size and number of parts. "You're turning a lot of metal. It's a complex system, but it's fun. I wouldn't want to work on any other plane."

B-1B pilots love the plane. USAF Captain Lucky (whose real name is disguised for security purposes) flew the B-1B for seven years before the war in Afghanistan. "It's a marvelous plane," he told the *Los Angeles Times*. "It's a fun airplane to fly," Lieutenant Colonel Garrett Harencak, 28th Bomb Squadron commander at Dyess Air Force Base, Texas, told *Airman*. Harencak runs the "schoolhouse" where new pilots and weapons officers receive their training.

"Those who fly it for the first time get a smile on their faces that stays on for the whole flight," says Harencak. "This airplane is just getting better and better. We're just scratching the surface of what this plane can do."

The B-1B holds sixty-one world records for speed, payload, and distance. The National Aeronautic Association honored the Lancer for completing one of the ten most memorable record flights for 1994. Over the years, it has become a more versatile plane—able to deliver a wide variety of precision-guided bombs and missiles as well as conventional cluster bombs—while also becoming more stealthy and skilled at slipping undetected into enemy airspace. The Lancer can carry more weapons and fly faster than either the B-52 or B-2. It has been the workhorse of the air force's bomber fleet in Afghanistan and scored major successes there, as well as in Iraq and Kosovo.

These satellite images show the destruction of Al Qaeda and Taliban positions in Afghanistan after they were struck by missiles from B-1B and B-52 bombers.

Despite all this, the Lancer's future remains very cloudy and uncertain. Even its longtime supporters do not expect it to be flying twenty years from now.

Only three months before the September 11, 2001, attacks, the U.S. Department of Defense and Congress were considering retiring a

This picture shows several B-1B Lancers flying in formation. The United States's war on terror has demonstrated the advantages of keeping and upgrading the B-1B fleet, leading military experts and aerospace industry pundits to predict that the warplanes will continue to be used in combat for many years to come.

third of the ninety-two B-1B bombers in service and stripping them of parts for use in the surviving sixty planes. The B-1Bs would be housed in two, rather than five, bases. The money saved would be used to support the remaining B-1B fleet. Congress has not yet approved this proposal, and the world has changed drastically since it was first made.

The war on terror may have extended the life of the B-1B. No Lancers are going to be grounded as long as the war on terror continues. In fact, Boeing Aircraft has received a $4.5 billion contract to make the B-1B the most effective high-tech, long-range bomber for use in combating the new enemies faced by the United States: international terrorists.

The future of the B-1B bomber will lie in its ability to fulfill the kinds of missions that have emerged in the post–September 11 world. Several new kinds of smart bombs and missiles are in development that will make it easier to target small clusters of terrorists hidden within crowded residential areas or vast, empty, featureless deserts. The B-1B's defensive and offensive avionics systems will also be improved, featuring global positioning system (GPS) technology that will allow the bomber to both identify enemy targets with greater precision and deliver bombs straight to them. Scheduled modifications will allow the B-1B to drop various kinds of weapons simultaneously from its three weapons bays (such as cluster bombs, cruise missiles, and JDAM guided bombs).

Colonel Christopher Miller, who oversees B-1B flying operations at Dyess Air Force Base, believes the upgrades will increase the usefulness of an already useful aircraft. He told the *Abilene*

The B-1B Lancer is a multipurpose, long-range bomber that can carry up to 50,000 pounds of armament. It reaches speeds of up to 900 miles per hour and has a wingspan, with wings swept fully forward, of 137 feet (41.8 meters). When the Lancer's wings are swept forward, as they are during takeoff, landing, and high-altitude cruising, the plane has greater maneuverability at low speeds.

*Reporter-News*, "We definitely need the new technology . . . That will make a huge improvement in our capability. Of course, we think we're pretty capable already."

Thanks largely to the new demands of the war against terror and the resulting changes to the B-1B and its mission, the Lancer seems to be in no immediate danger of retirement. Though one of the main players in the success of Operation Enduring Freedom, it still remains an aircraft that generates great controversy. The B-1B has endured almost forty years of criticism and threats of cancellation, yet it continues to take to the skies. As U.S. Representative Charles Stenholm told the *Abilene Reporter-News*, "No one in the Air Force believes there is any other plane that is the backbone of the bomber force but the B-1. Nobody.

"The B-1 is not a perfect airplane. It never has been. But it is the best we've got."

**Al Qaeda** The terrorist group led by Osama bin Laden that attacked the United States on September 11, 2001. In Arabic, Al Qaeda means "the base." It is believed to have members operating secretly in over sixty countries around the world.

**armament** The military term for offensive weapons, such as guns, bombs, and missiles.

**bomb** An explosive device that is delivered from the air to ground or sea targets. Bombs are dropped; they do not fly under their own power like missiles do.

**Cold War** The conflict between the United States and the former Soviet Union that lasted from 1946 to 1991. It was called a cold war because no actual battles were fought.

**conventional weapons** Bombs or missiles that use non-nuclear explosives and do not poison the environment with radiation after they explode.

**flight crew** The people who fly an aircraft. In the B-1B, the flight crew consists of the mission commander, the copilot, the offensive weapons officer, and the defensive weapons officer.

**global positioning system (GPS)** A technology that uses satellites high in space to provide the exact location of enemy targets, making bomb and missile attacks of pinpoint accuracy possible.

**JDAM (joint direct attack munition) bomb** An ordinary bomb that is fitted with an instrument that allows it to be guided to its target (rather than simply dropped on or near it) by crews in the air or on the ground.

**missile** An explosive weapon that is launched from sea, air, or land to reach its target. Missiles have their own propulsion system and fly on their own power to their targets.

*nuclear weapons*  Bombs or missiles that contain radioactive material that can explode with huge force; also called weapons of mass destruction. Many treaties forbid their use. Their explosive force is measured in kilotons. A kiloton is the equivalent of 1,000 tons of TNT. The atomic bomb dropped on Hiroshima, Japan, by the United States on August 6, 1945, released 12.5 kilotons of energy.

*prototype*  An early version of a product, such as a plane, that is used for testing and development. The B-1A was the prototype of the B-1B Lancer.

*smart bomb*  Any bomb or missile that uses global positioning system (GPS) technology, radar, or other technology to be guided during its flight to its target; a smart bomb can change direction mid-flight on the orders of crews on the ground or in the air.

*sortie*  The military name for an individual mission that is flown by one aircraft to achieve a specific military goal. If a mission involves the use of twelve aircraft, there have been twelve sorties.

*stealth technology*  Using special anti-radar technology and advanced avionics to "fool" enemy radar on the ground or in the air, making a plane extremely difficult to detect.

*strategic*  The military term used to describe long-range or long-term goals.

*terrorist*  A member of a political group that is organized to achieve its political goals through attacking, frightening, and intimidating innocent civilians. Terrorist tactics include hijacking planes, planting bombs, suicide bombings, and sniper attacks.

*war on terror*  The name given by U.S. president George W. Bush for the long-term, worldwide conflict begun against terrorism following the terrorist attacks in the United States on September 11, 2001.

# FOR MORE INFORMATION

Air Force Historical Research Agency
600 Chennault Circle
Building 1405
Maxwell AFB, AL 36112-6424
(334) 953-2395
Web site: http://www.au.af.mil/au/afhra

Air Force Research Laboratory
Public Affairs Office
1864 4th Street
Building 15, Room 225
WPAFB, OH 45433-7131
Web site: http://www.afrl.af.mil

*Air Force Times*
Army Times Publishing Co.
6883 Commercial Drive
Springfield, VA 22159-0500
Web site: http://www.airforcetimes.com

Boeing Military Aircraft and Missile Systems
P.O. Box 516
St. Louis, MO 63166
(314) 232-0232
Web site: http://www.boeing.com

National Air and Space Museum
7th and Independence Avenue SW
Washington, DC 20560
Web site: http://www.nasm.si.edu

U.S. Air Force Academy
HQ, USAFA
Colorado Springs, CO 80840
Web site: http://www.usafa.af.mil/noflash/index.html

U.S. Air Force Air Combat Command
Public Affairs Office
115 Thompson Street, Suite 211
Langley AFB, VA 23665-1987
Web site: http://www2.acc.af.mil/index.stml

U.S. Air Force Museum
1100 Spaatz Street
Wright-Patterson AFB, OH 45433
(937) 255-3286
Web site: http://www.wpafb.af.mil/museum/index.htm

U.S. Air Force Public Affairs Resource Library
1690 Air Force Pentagon
Washington, DC 20330-1690
Web site: http://www.af.mil

## Web Sites

Due to the changing nature of Internet links, the Rosen Publishing Group, Inc., has developed an online list of Web sites related to the subject of this book. This site is updated regularly. Please use this link to access the list:

http://www.rosenlinks.com/usw/lanc/

# FOR FURTHER READING

Chant, Christopher. *The Role of the Fighter Bomber*. New York: Chelsea House, 1999.

Dougherty, Terri. *The U.S. Air Force at War.* Mankato, MN: Capstone Press, 2001.

Green, Michael. *The United States Air Force.* Mankato, MN: Capstone Press, 1998.

Hamilton, John. *Operation Enduring Freedom.* Edina, MN: ABDO Publishing Co., 2002.

Landau, Elaine. *Osama bin Laden: A War Against the West.* Breckenridge, CO: 21st Century Books, Inc., 2002.

Langley, Wanda. *The Air Force in Action*. New York: Enslow Publishers, 2001.

Schleifer, Jay. *Bomber Planes.* Mankato, MN: Capstone Press, 1996.

Taylor, David. *The Cold War.* Crystal Lake, IL: Heinemann Library, 2001.

# BIBLIOGRAPHY

Air Education Training and Command. "Joint Specialized Undergraduate Pilot Training." USAF Fact Sheet. May 2001. Retrieved February 2002 (http://www.af.mil/news/factsheets/ Joint_Specialized_Pilot.html).

Air Force Technology Projects. "B-1B Lancer Strategic Bomber." The Website for Defence Industries, Air Force. 2002. Retrieved March 2002 (http://www.airforce-technology.com/projects/b-1b/).

Biggerstaff, Msgt. Jim. "One Hot Bomber." *Airman*. August 2000. Retrieved February 2002 (http://www.af.mil/news/airman/ 0800/bomber2.htm).

Burns, Robert. "Crew Safe After Bomber Goes Down." Newsday.com. December 13, 2001. Retrieved February 2002 (http://www. newsday.com/news/nationworld/sns-worldtrade-bomber.story? coll=ny-top-span-headlines).

Donnini, Frank P. *Battling for Bombers: The U.S. Air Force Fights for Its Modern Strategic Aircraft Programs.* Westport, CT: Greenwood Publishing Group, 2000.

Federation of American Scientists. "B-1B Lancer." Weapons of Mass Destruction Around the World. October 1999. Retrieved February 2002 (http://www.fas.org/nuke/guide/usa/bomber/b-1b.htm).

GlobalSecurity.org. "B-1B Losses." December 2001. Retrieved February 2002 (http://www.globalsecurity.org/wmd/systems/ b-1b-loss.htm).

Jenkins, Dennis R. *The B-1B Lancer: The Most Complicated Warplanes Ever Developed*. New York: McGraw-Hill, 1999.

Kotz, Nick. *Wild Blue Yonder: Money, Politics and the B-1 Bomber.* New York: Pantheon Books, 1988.

Lambeth, Benjamin S. *The Transformation of American Air Power.* Ithaca, NY: Cornell University Press, 2000.

Logan, Don. *Rockwell B-1B: SAC's Last Bomber.* Atglen, PA: Schiffer Publishing, Ltd., 1995.

Lorell, Mark A. *The Cutting Edge: A Half Century of U.S. Fighter R&D.* Santa Monica, CA: The Rand Corporation, 1998.

Milburn, John. "Flight of the B-1B." *Morning Sun.* January 7, 2002. Retrieved February 2002 (http://www.morningsun.net/stories/010702/loc_0107020022.shtml).

Pae, Peter. "Maligned B-1 Bomber Now Proving Its Worth." *Los Angeles Times.* December 12, 2001. Retrieved March 2002 (http://www.globalsecurity.org/org/news/2001/011212-attack02.htm).

Pournelle, Jerry. Chairman, Citizen's Advisory Council on National Space Policy. Personal interview with author. December 29, 2001.

Schuhmann, Sidney. "Air Force: B-1 Safe Despite Problems." *Abilene Reporter-News.* December 20, 2001. Retrieved May 2002 (http://www.reporternews.com/2001/local/bone1220.html).

Schuhmann, Sidney. "Criticism of B-1 Is Not New." *Abilene Reporter-News.* July 15, 2001. Retrieved May 2002 (http://www.texnews.com/1998/2001/local/new0715.html).

Schuhmann, Sidney. "Pentagon Mum on B-1 Record." *Abilene Reporter-News.* November 29, 2001. Retrieved May 2002 (http://www.reporternews.com/2001/local/bone1129.html).

USAF Fact Sheet. "B-1B Lancer." July 2001. Retrieved February 2002 (http://www.af.mil/news/factsheets/B_1B_Lancer.html).

# INDEX

## About the Author

Amy Sterling Casil is a Southern California resident. She teaches at Saddleback College in Mission Viejo and is a Nebula Award–nominated science fiction writer. She enjoys spending time with her daughter, friends, students, and Jack Russell terrier, Badger.

## Photo Credits

Cover, pp. 4, 13, 32, 37 © David Halford; pp. 5, 14 © Reuters NewMedia, Inc./Corbis; pp. 6, 9, 23, 36 © AFP/Corbis; p. 10 © Bettmann/Corbis; p. 16 © George Hall/Corbis; p. 18 © Sgt. Kenneth Fidler/U.S. Air Force; p. 21 © U.S. Air Force; pp. 24–25, 26 © TimePix; p. 29 © AP/Wide World Photos; p. 30 © Sgt. Randy Mallard/U.S. Air Force; p. 33 © Corbis; p. 35 © U.S. Dept. of Defense/TimePix.

## Editor

John Kemmerer

## Layout and Design

Tom Forget